A-MAZE-ING FACES

This book belongs to:

____

Created by @Rebekah Baht-Israel

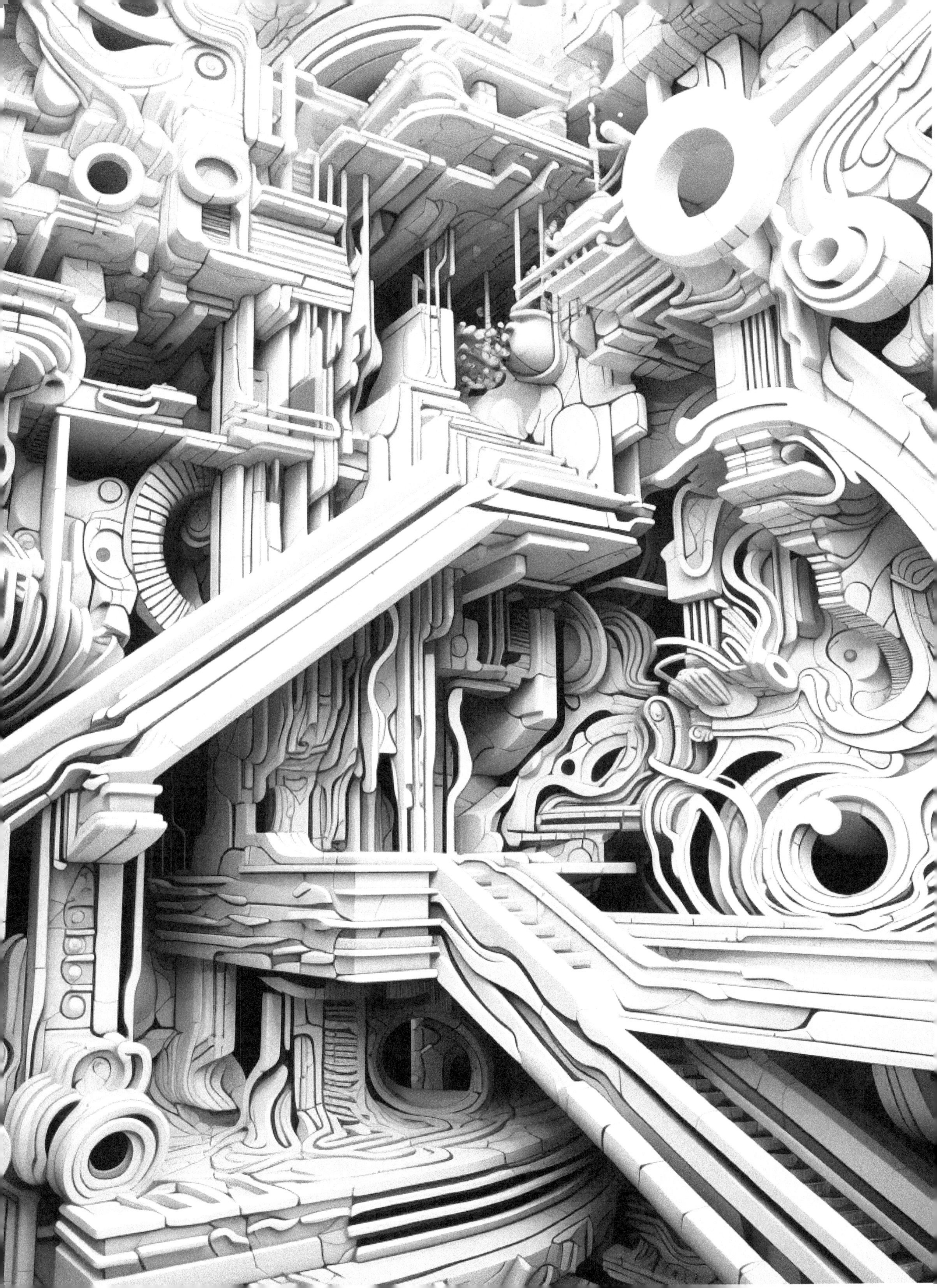

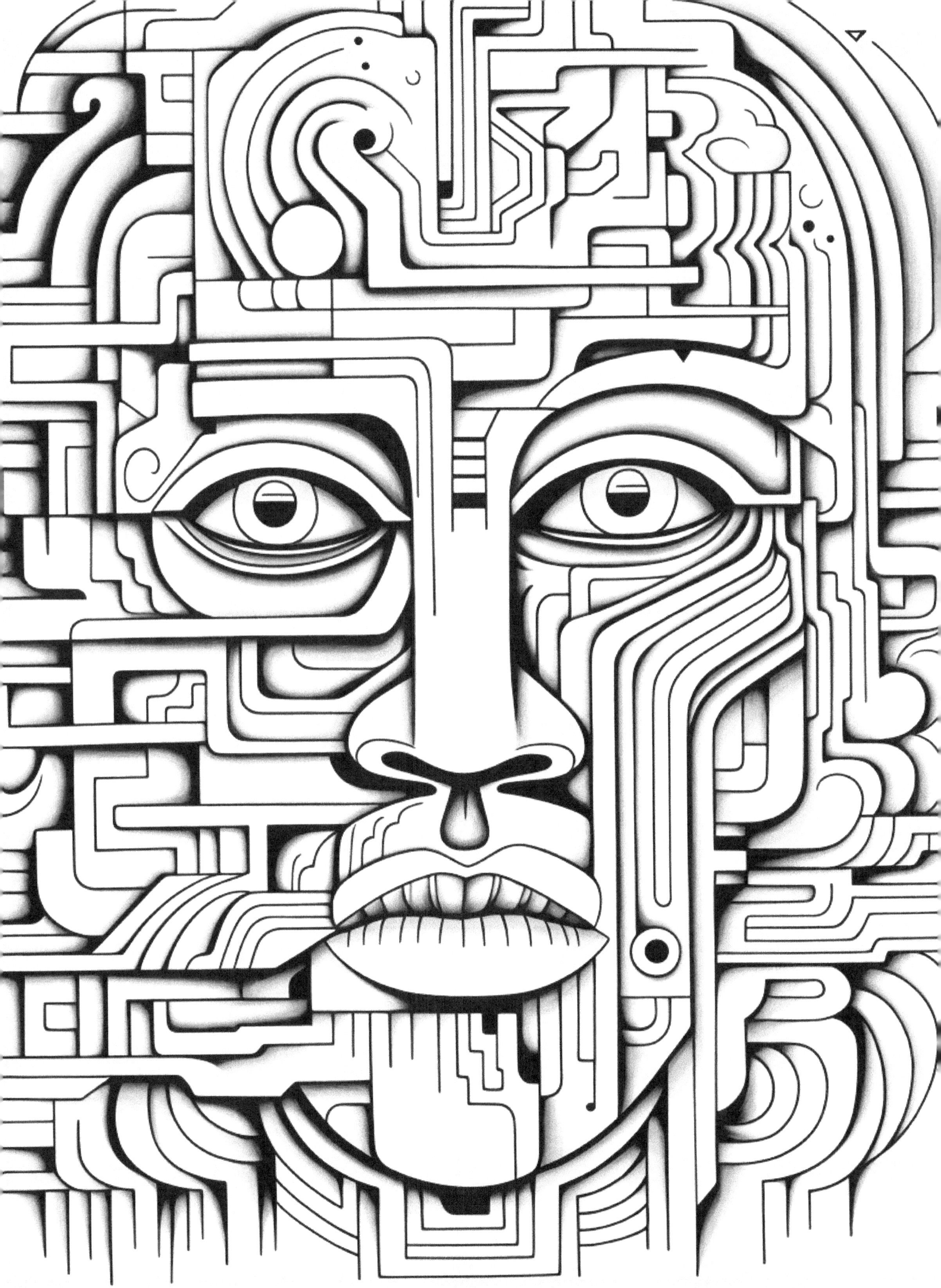

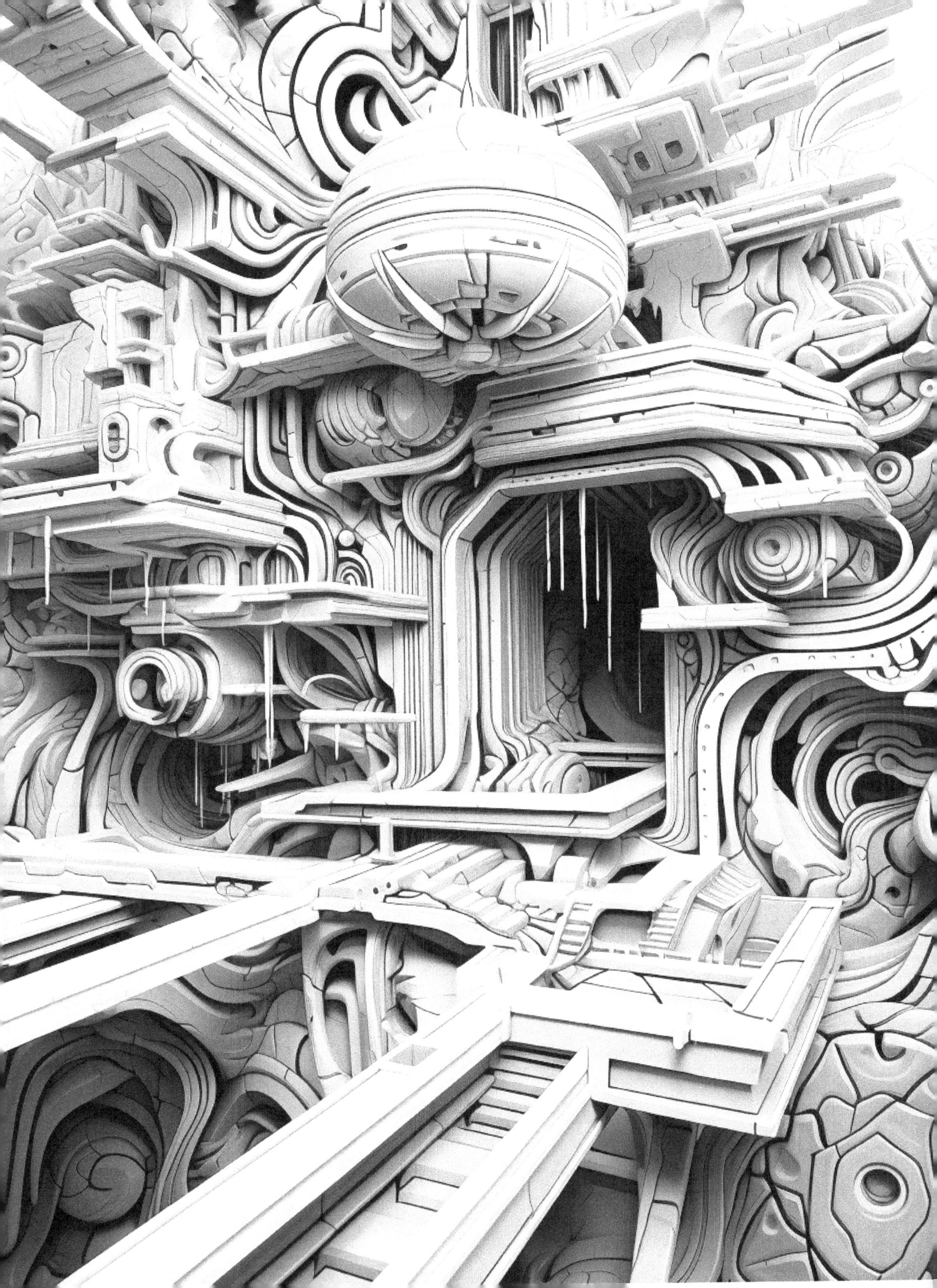

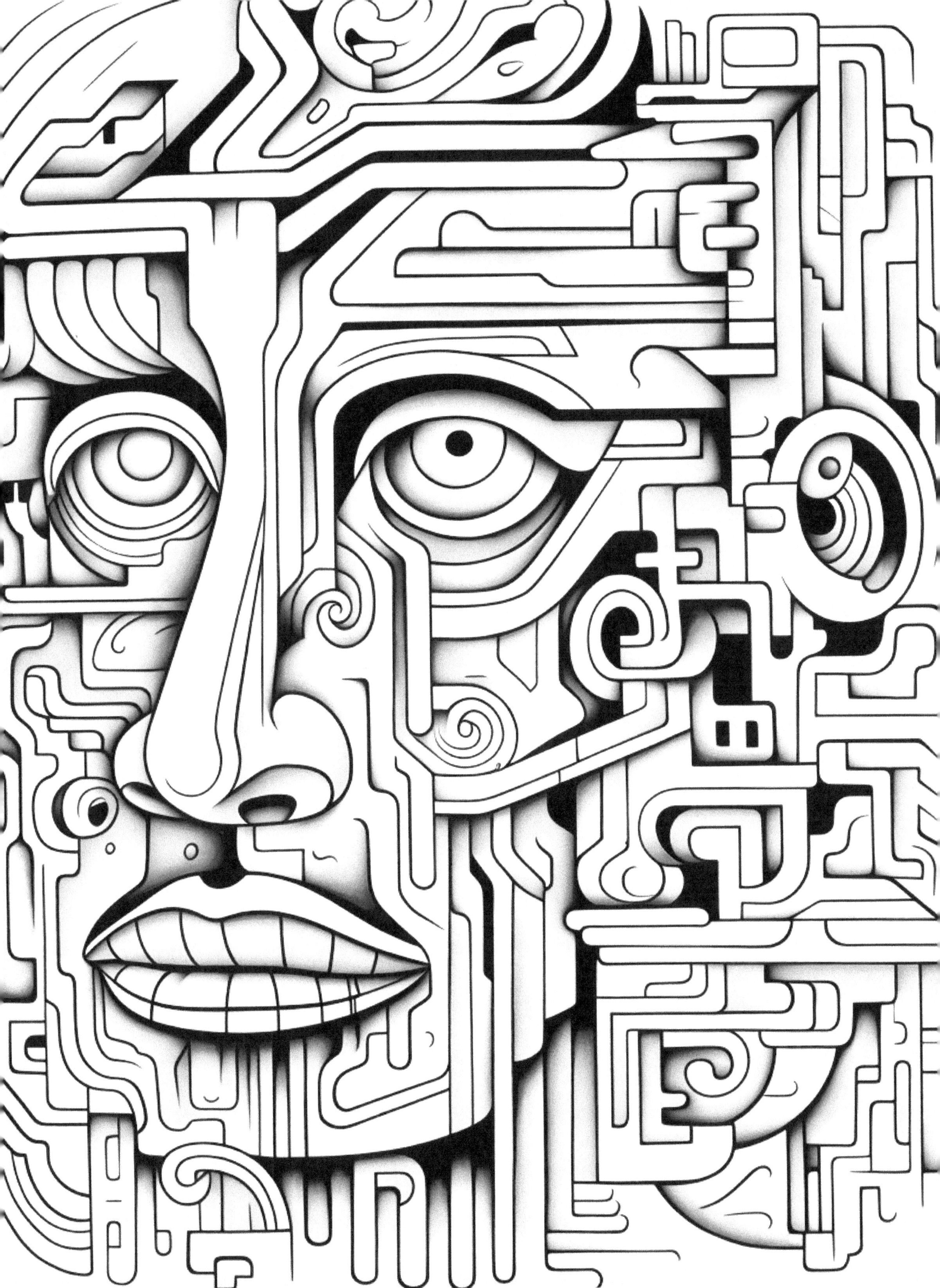

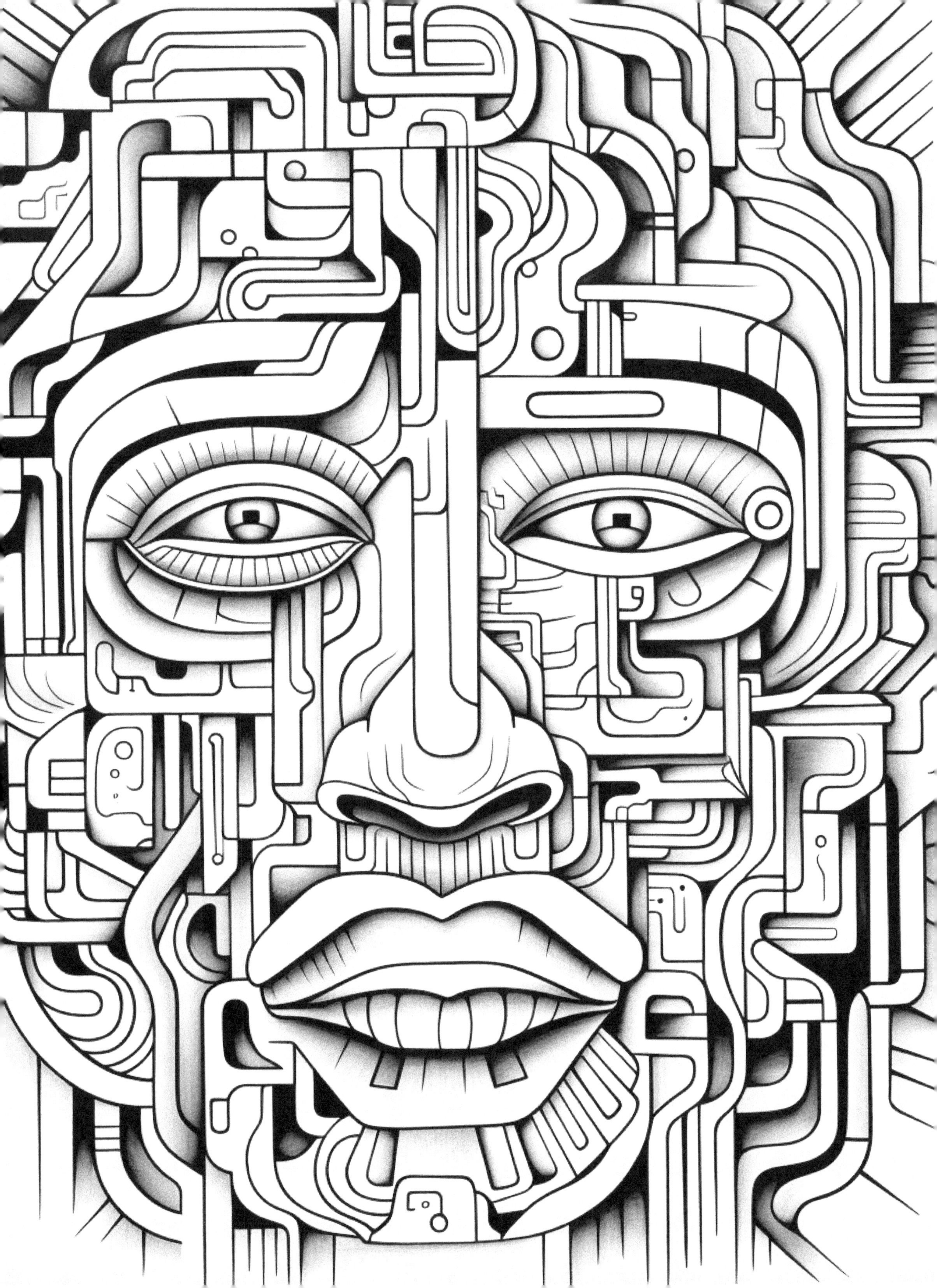